MW01168365

BROKEN for the Anointing

Chardoneé Wright

Broken

All rights reserved. No part of this book may be used or reproduced by any means, graphic, electronic, or mechanical, including photocopying, recording, taping, or by any information storage retrieval system without the written permission of Anointed Ink Publishing except in the case of brief quotations embodied in critical articles and reviews.

Scripture taken from the New King James Version®. Copyright © 1982 by Thomas Nelson. Used by permission. All rights reserved

Copyright 2015,

Anointed Ink Publishing

PO Box 1424

Highland, NY 12528

ISBN: 978-1515063742

Control: 2015943382

I would like to dedicate this book to my heavenly Father. Thank you for never giving up on me, continually leading and guiding me towards the woman I am today. You have shown yourself mighty and strong throughout my life and I bless you. May all and full glory belong to you. Because you've given me this testimony, this is my gift back to you. This book is also dedicated to my Pastor and spiritual mother, Dr. Racquel Stroud. Thank you for believing in me and taking the time to walk me through my healing and deliverance.

Table of Contents

Chapter One

6

Chapter Two

21

Chapter Three

29

Chapter Four

47

Dedication

63

Rededication

65

Letter to God

66

I was broken and incomplete. My heart was shattered and fragmented. The deception of unworthiness kept me in a self-inflicted prison. The wounds of my past were iron bars encamping around my mind. The deceptive lies of satan kept me at a distance from my God, my Creator. Through my brokenness, I learned of the extraordinary love of Jesus Christ and the great extent of His mercy and grace. My brokenness propelled and prepared me to walk in the anointing and calling God has placed on my life. This is my story.

Chapter One

Help Me, Lord

I was afraid of God, truly petrified.

I didn't understand that He was the epitome of true, authentic love. I would read the Old Testament and saw the ways that He punished people and that was the only side that I chose to see. I ran from God and kept running, even while in the church. I barely wanted to be alone with Him, and when I was alone with God, I wanted our alone time to go my way. I used control and manipulation as a weapon to guard my heart from being hurt. My limited perspective about God damaged our relationship. I didn't honor and reverence Him as the King of Kings and Lord of Lords. I thought God was on my terms and I tried to control and manipulate Him; which was wrong. I went through a long season of my life where my heart was hardened.

Ever been in a place where the pain of life seemed so unbearable? How did you deal with it?

I dealt with my pain by isolating myself, but in the meantime, my heart turned cold and stony. Because of this, the love of God was not able to fully penetrate into my heart the way it was supposed to. I had wires and fences around my heart against God because of what people did to me.

Isolation was the worst solution because it opened the door to the demonic realm and I was mentally tormented by demons day after day after day. I was double-minded and unstable in all of my ways. I was tossed to and fro like a wave of the sea.

"But let him ask in faith, with no doubting, for he who doubts is like a wave of the sea driven and tossed by the wind. For let not that man suppose that he will receive anything from the Lord; he is a double-minded man, unstable in all his ways."
James 1:6-8 NKJV

I became so acquainted with this condition, that I believed that this was normal. I didn't see happiness, all I saw was despair. I didn't have faith, I carried doubt around in my purse.

Doubt was rooted deep into my heart. I didn't have joy or peace, I constantly worried about everything. Money was my God and my idol. My personal ambitions and dreams drowned out God's voice and I walked heavily in the spirit of pride.

When I first stepped out on launching Woman, I Am Incorporated, I was so scared. I had no clue how to run a business and had not taken any formal business training classes. My background was in journalism. However, something deep down inside of me knew that this was the right thing to do. That inner prompting was called "purpose." You are called to solve some problems in the world and you will attract certain people to you because you went through the same thing. I attracted a lot of women who were just like me.

I had no clue WIA was called to be an international ministry. It was merely a workshop that I had in mind that eventually became a support group, then business, then a nonprofit and it kept progressing. When I stepped out in blind faith to pursue this adventure, I had no clue what I was getting into. The first year of launching WIA, I was sick with the flu and was very sick spiritually.

I had a lot of opposition and would often go home and cry to my mother. Sometimes 3-4 people would show up, but I still did my best as if it were a crowd of women in our meetings. I worked the night shift until 11 pm and would be up early the next morning cleaning, decorating and preparing our meeting space for the women and go back to work the same night. At this time, we were evicted out of our home and family of six moved to a one bedroom apartment. That was tough. It was three of us to a bed and I ran WIA out of the trunk of my car. The second year of WIA, my little brother was shot in his head two weeks before our annual orientation. While he was laying in the intensive care unit, I had to continue to be strong for the women who needed me. Ministry didn't stop because I was going through tribulations. It was then that I began to break. I began to cry out to God to help me. My brother was fighting for my life, I had an entire organization to run and I was still in graduate school. My testimony is one about endurance and how an incredible God strengthened me in my weakest moments and taught me that in order to be used by Him, the anointing had to be authentic, therefore I had to be broken.

As a younger girl, I was hurt, rejected, abandoned, teased, bullied, controlled and manipulated. By the time I began high school, I had no identity. I was trying to wear the identity of other women. I wanted to be like the "popular girls" who would receive all of the attention from men; I never saw my value. I felt worthless but would try to hide it. In high school and college, I had a few boyfriends but deep down inside, I really wanted a father. So, in essence; these "boyfriends" resembled a father-like figure to me because they would give me the attention that my heart craved.

They would tell me that I was beautiful and validated me through words and actions. My gullible frame at the time would do any and everything to keep my relationships together because without a "relationship," I felt unworthy. I was unable to see the beauty bestowed upon me by God because I acquainted beauty with outside appearance and intimacy with sex.

However, I've learned that there is a greater beauty that God gives His children and intimacy with God isn't about having goose- bumps all over your body. God is not a "feeling." Nor can we ever compare the love that He has for us with a man or woman's love. I blatantly disrespected God by not believing in me the way that He believes in me.

It's a dangerous place to be in when you put your validation and worth in worthless things and people. People are flawed and subject to fail and disappoint you. It's inevitable. We do it all the time to others. We hurt each other's feelings without knowing it or caring, we haven't always kept our word or lived up to the standards of others. Face it, we are subject to miss it because we are human. However, I am not condoning it, but what I am saying is that we have to know our limitations as humans and how God made us. In our weakness, His power is made perfected (2 Corinthians 12:9)

It's in our lowest state where God can truly begin that good work in you. You have to want God. He is a gentleman and will not force Himself on you, but you must invite Him in.

"Behold, I stand at the door and knock. If anyone hears My voice and opens the door, I will come in to him and dine with him, and he with Me.

"Revelation 3:20

My heart was sorrowful when I thought about how many times my attitudes, thoughts, behaviors, and heart rejected Jesus. How patient Jesus is with us, constantly pursuing us, constantly in the corner watching and waiting. He waits on His bride, no matter what you've done, it's never too late to come back to Him.

Who is this king of Glory? Who is this man who has loved my aching heart so much? Who is this Jesus? Is He a figment of my imagination? No, He is the king of kings and savior of the world. Jesus is real. Jesus really cares about you. If no one else cares about you, He does.

Jesus doesn't look at the outside appearance as man does, but He knows the very melodies of our hearts. He knows our getting up and our lying down. He was there when we were being intricately crafted in the wombs of our mothers. (Jeremiah 1:5)

Jesus is the beginning and the end. If you would open your heart to Him and not be afraid, He will come in and fill it with joy, peace, happiness and authentic love.

It was hard for me to develop a relationship with God at first because my natural father wasn't around. I didn't have a male figure in the home beside my little brother, and I couldn't comprehend what the role of a Father truly was. If I wanted something, I had to work for it. I didn't know how to ask for help.

I didn't believe that God cared for me. I viewed myself as just a speck in a world full of people. I felt that no one paid any attention to me and I had to go over and beyond to gain the attention of others. That opened the gates for the spirit of pride to come in, because I acquainted my achievements and accomplishments with my identity.

As I developed a relationship with God, it was startling to me at first of all the promises that He has made me and I would expect God to let me down, because I experienced that with my earthly father. God was just so good to me that I thought it was some trick to the Christian walk.

When a father is taken out of the home for any reason, the original family dynamic is shifted because fathers/husbands are ordained by God to be the head of the household. The enemy knows that if he can sift the father and take him out, then the entire family would suffer. A man has to give an account to God for everything that bears his last name. Therefore, if the enemy can shoot the head down (father) than everything under him would crumble. Women were never designed to bear the weight that husbands/fathers have.

As I matured, I realized the spiritual implications behind this. Outwardly, a man could be viewed as a deadbeat, in jail, on drugs or whatever circumstances he is in, but what about the hearts of the men? Inwardly, many men are hurt, broken, were abandoned and are just repeating the cycles that they experienced in their home or that trickled down from their generational bloodline. Some men were never taught how to be men of God because someone didn't teach their father. So, we end up with a generation of fatherless women and men who turn to other outlets to fill a void that can't be filled through human efforts. It has to be filled by God.

In my underdevelopment, I could not fathom how a God that lives in heaven would truly want a relationship with me. After all, wasn't He busy saving the world? Didn't He have other things to do beside help me in my despair?

My limited view of God was improper and it cost me. If I can spare someone else from believing this way and wasting time, I hope that I can. I wasted a lot of valuable time believing the lies of satan. I've wasted valuable time choosing not to believe that I was truly a daughter of the King. I wasted valuable time not fully understanding that on that same cross that Jesus died for sinners, that I, yes even I, was counted in the number.

On the outside, I was growing into a woman, but on the inside I found myself spiritually underdeveloped in certain areas. My spirit was thirsty for Jesus but I didn't understand. I looked to find love in so many different places. I just wanted to be accepted for who I was. I wanted to be validated by people, but when I became disappointed or people failed me, my heart hardened. I put people on a pedestal and made idols out of relationships. I thought fulfillment came through worldly possessions, statuses and accomplishments. I was sadly mistaken. This void that I felt, this darkness that I was living in could only be penetrated by the light of Christ, the Savior of the world.

Simply put, LIGHT illuminates. Light is the form of energy that makes is possible to see things. Without light, you can't see. Without light, you are in the dark. Without light, you aren't able to separate night from day. Light drives out darkness. It also plays many roles in our everyday lives. Flashlights, chandeliers, light bulbs — all illuminate -- but the greatest beam of light is the magnificent radiance of Jesus Christ. Jesus gleams with beauty. Jesus is the greatest light agent that makes all things visible to those living in the darkness. His very being holds the true essence of life. He is the light of life, and whoever is a follower of Christ will walk in the light with Him. The luminosity of Jesus outshines even the brightest star in the sky. Christ's light is so commanding and powerful, that it is able to take an evil person with the darkest past and transform them from the inside out. Jesus Christ strips away the dark layers, searches the depths of your heart, and sees the real you.

"Then Jesus spoke to them again, saying, "I am the light of the world. He who follows Me shall not walk in darkness, but have the light of life."

John 8:12

I would not trade my past in for the world, because it taught me perseverance, strength, and endurance. When you look at your past, how many things do you wish didn't happen? How many times do you wish your mother or father were there to support you or to love you? Have you ever considered that perhaps God orchestrated it this way because He knew that you had to go through some things in order to have a testimony? In order to have a song in your heart, a book to write, a sermon to preach, you have to go through tests, trials and tribulations.

These are the very foundations to birth out the greatness that is hidden deep within the depths of your soul. What if God allowed your mother/father to be in your life and they hindered you? What if God was protecting you from something that you couldn't understand or comprehended? Doesn't God know best? What is He trying to teach and birth out of you? What lessons are you supposed to learn? We have to ask ourselves these questions. If God works all things out for our good, no matter what it is, then there has to be good in every situation; even a broken past.

Although our outside bodies continue to develop, there may still remain an inner young boy or young girl who is trapped in time. Your story may be different. Perhaps your father and/or mother wasn't absent from your life. Maybe they were present physically, but didn't provide the proper emotional or mental attention needed for you to develop as a child.

Maybe no one ever told you that you were loved, worthy and precious. Perhaps you were stripped of intimacy and affection. Whatever your story may be today, God wants to heal you.

I was emotionally damaged at a young age, therefore I stayed stuck in that moment of time. By God's undeniable grace, patience, pastoral intervention, counsel, and with much prayer; I was able to move from that place that I was underdeveloped in.

I'm not promising you a bed of roses, nor is this book written to tickle your ears. You will have to make painful decisions when you chose to follow Christ. It will hurt and the road to healing is not a walk in the park, but it is rewarding. If you truly want to be healed and restored completely, it will not happen overnight. You've been carrying that weight for a long time; maybe even your entire life. Those wounds are now bleeding and you can no longer keep changing the Band Aid hoping that it would eventually go away.

Pain left undetected and untreated is dangerous, but the first step to walking into your destiny is opening your heart to Christ.

Chapter Two

Take Off Your Mask

In order to heal, you have to be exposed. How can you expect to move forward if you don't want God to show you what demonic spirits has taken its position in your house? You've worn this mask for too long, now it's time to get to the real you, your authentic self. Your authentic identity lies in Christ alone and the lies of the enemy have been sown into your heart to make you unfruitful. If you continue to walk in unfruitfulness because of undetected pain, God is going to deal with you.

Every day, people are dying and going to hell, and you are still upset about what your mother and father did to you in your past. At what point is it going to be enough? You may be called to be an apostle to bring governmental order on the earth, but you can't see past the rape or molestation.

You may be called to be a Pastor and lead God's sheep, you may be called to be an evangelist to win souls for the Lord, you may be called to be a prophet of God to declare what Thus says the Lord. You may be called to be a teacher to edify the body of Christ, but you don't want to move past yesterday and you won't allow God to heal you. You must take time for yourself; Take time

to heal. Slow down, sit down somewhere, and receive instruction,

wisdom, and knowledge from God; the book of Proverbs is full of

it.   There are souls and lives that are waiting of you to get in

position and be all that God has called you to be.

When I was younger, I remember the night my house was

raided by police officers and my sister and I had to duck low in a

room while the police went through all of my mom's personal

belongings; Papers were everywhere. Drawers were half hanging

out of its shelves. Then, I remember moving and having no place

to go. It was then that we moved to my grandmother's house. As

a young girl, I didn't fully understand what was going on.

I wore plenty of masks to conceal my inner pain. I was

beyond great at covering things up. In fact, I was the master of

covering things up. As a child, I grew up without luxurious

things. I wore hand me downs and my mother did her best to

provide a great, quality life. To me, the world was a stage and I was the leading actress. Fake smiles and lies were my cover up as I tried to keep my friends out of my personal life.

My grandmother was the apple of my eye. Growing up, my siblings and I were always under my grandmother's wings. She trained us, disciplined us, and helped us in all ways possible. My life changed drastically when she passed. I was sad and hurt. Why did we move? What was going on? Living with my grandmother was one of the toughest things I ever had to do in my life. Before she passed away, we moved in with her to help take care of her. However, my family tightly squeezed into a small home. I didn't know what it was like at this moment to have anything to myself, everything was shared with my siblings. I used the kitchen closet to store my belongings in plastic trash bags. No space. My bed was a couch, covered in plastic. Imagine one bedroom, six people, a living room and kitchen that were within inches of each other.

I would grab a sheet and pillow and lay it across the couch and that would be my bed for the night. The most rewarding nights were when I was able to sleep next to grandma in her comfy bed and watch television. She was quiet at night, but I would be so thankful I literally had a bed to sleep in, that it wouldn't matter. My mom and brother and sisters slept on the air mattress at night. Everyone huddled together to get a good night sleep or get part of a cover.

Some people knew we stayed there, some didn't. Some guessed we did, but couldn't imagine the conditions we were in. Don't get me wrong, I enjoyed at least having somewhere to stay, but as a young girl, I was embarrassed about my living conditions. At school, every one of my friends had big fancy houses with pools and big back yards; I didn't'. I felt lonely, as if in a world of my own. Why did I live that way and my friends didn't? I was in a state of denial, anger, and rage. I didn't have the latest fashion clothes, jewelry, and shoes all the time. At this point in my life I believe I developed low self-esteem; Smiling on the outside, but hurt, broken and torn on the inside.

Because of my inner hurt, I began to pour myself into my studies and school to fill this void. I attended a magnet school from 4th-8th grade and that was one of the greatest blessings I've ever experienced.

I was always in the TAG (Talented. And. Gifted) programs, school plays, and other activities. But, after the programs ended and school was done for the day, I went back to my home and tucked my mask away in my drawer, ready to put it back on the next day. Behind this mask is where I felt protected but I couldn't keep covering everything up. Eventually, others were going to find out our living conditions and I was afraid that if you knew the real me, you wouldn't like me.

I wanted to be everyone's friend because I genuinely loved people. I wanted to see everyone happy. My self-image was so tattered and torn that I believed that I had to win people over and go the extra mile just to have a friend. My validation was in people. If I took my mask off, would you still love me? If I opened myself up to you, would you value me?

Do you have on any mask? Do you hide and cover things up? I'm not saying go to the world and tell them all of your business, but what I am saying is that the same behavior that you exhibit in the natural will manifest in the spiritual. And so again, this cover up cost me. As in the natural, so in the spiritual.

I would cover up so many sins in the natural that I also "attempted to cover up" before God. God desires us spiritually naked and unashamed. He wants us to come to Him confessing, repenting and humbling ourselves. Such was the same as with Adam and Eve. When they sinned before the Lord, they were aware of their nakedness and sowed fig leaves together to try to hide and conceal their nakedness. How similar we can be, as if God doesn't already know everything about us.

"Then the eyes of both of them were opened, and they knew that they were naked; and they sewed fig leaves together and made themselves coverings." Genesis 3:7

He wants us to be free from sin and healed from the inside, out. If you find yourself so used to covering things up, you will never fully and freely walk in your freedom. I have found such beauty in repentance because it shows just how much you have to depend on God. It shows you that God has given us another chance and that you don't have to hide from Him because He is not mad at you. It shows you that despite all of your imperfections and flaws, God can still use you. You are not disqualified to be used by God because of what happened to you. You are not a piece of junk, and you are not trash. You are worthy and validated in your Father's eyes. At what point are you going to be whom God has called you to be? At what point will you fully surrender with a blind "yes" and give God your all? What are you afraid of? Are you afraid of people's opinion? Do they have a heaven or hell to put you in? Did these people take 39 lashes on their back for you, carried a cross and were nailed to it for your freedom? Did they give you gifts and dreams? If the answer is no, then why is it that the opinion of people hold more weight than the opinion of the God who created you does? Something is wrong.

Chapter Three

The Day My Dreams Died

In my quest towards freedom and healing, my wings were broken, torn, cut and severed. My dreams were dying. My life was a blur.

I didn't know how I got to this place, but I knew I didn't want to remain there. In the middle of my personal metamorphosis from the nest to the sky something happened; Life happened, with its unpredictable twists and turns, I no longer wanted to fly. I no longer wanted to dream again.

But then, the very hand of my Creator, Lord and Father took His mighty hand and began to do a work in my heart. He sent me His love through my mother who saw past the hurt, pain, pride, and affliction and recognized an insecure, young girl at heart who was hurt and ready to give up. It was then that love began to lift me up.

The authentic love of God will heal the wounds and ease the pain. It brings comfort to the afflicted and hope to the lost. His love is beyond words and is so deep and wide, you can't even fathom it. The love that God shows towards us can't even be put into words. Who are we that God is mindful of us in all of our flaws and inadequacies? Who are we for God to love us the way that He does? We are His creation; that is who we are, His beloved children, His precious children of His womb, His offspring, the apple of His eyes, His sunshine, His sunflowers and His seed.

Through the purging, pruning and plucking of my healing process, this eagle began to dream again. My wings were no longer broken. They were put back together; not by glue but by love. Love healed my wings. They were no longer torn or severed; they were healed and ready to fly.

I would encourage every parent reading this book to help protect, nurture and develop the gifts and talents that your children carry. It is so important that children develop properly through the word of God (Proverbs 22:6) if your child is an artist and loves to paint or draw, buy them an easel and a paint set. If you recognize that your child loves to read, spend time with them at the library and buy them notebooks and pens. If your child loves science, help them invest in that area. Recognize what God

has put on the inside of them so that it won't die in the womb.

As a young girl, I was very ambitious. I used to read all

day, play school with my teddy bears and use my imagination all

the time. Because of this, I was teased, I was bullied, and I was

made fun of. I remember people constantly calling me "motor

mouth." But, I loved to express myself, talk and write. I didn't

understand why people would say mean things to me and I

would just love them and want to be everyone's friend.

I thought something was wrong with me. Was I the only

one with big dreams? Did anyone else see what I saw? I didn't

know when I was younger that I was a visionary for God.

Therefore, to the average person, I was weird. It doesn't matter

what people have to say about you, you have come to this earth

with gifts, talents, and dreams and if you are not careful, others

will shoot those dreams down. If you don't know who you really

are in Christ and what He requires of you, those dreams can die.

Do not give up on yourself. Be encouraged that God who has begun a good work in you is faithful to complete it. It is He who started the work and promises to see you to the end. Yes, life is not always easy, it can be painful, but you have to decide which day is going to be the new day for you. How long will your story be the reason why you are stagnant? At what point will your story help someone else? You cannot continue to use your story and past as a tool to play the victim card. Yes, it has happened to you and it hurt. But God is a healer and restorer who makes all things new.

"Therefore, if anyone is in Christ, he is a new creation; old things have passed away; behold, all things have become new."
2 Corinthians 5:17

Change your perspective about what happened to you. If you want to stay stuck where you are, then keep playing the victim role. If you want to move forward and advance the kingdom of God, you must decide right now that you will no longer use your past as a clutch, but use it as a testimony to propel you into your future and to maximize your potential.

When I was in middle school, the Lord allowed me to excel academically, so I was put in the higher classes by myself, while my friends weren't. I wanted to be with my friends, I wanted to be where they were, so I would dumb myself down to try and fit in. As I did this naturally, I began to do this spiritually. I wasn't walking in my authority, nor did I believe in the God in me to use such a girl to accomplish incredible exploits. My identity was so attached to people that I refused to walk in what God had for me because I didn't believe.

Do you know who you really are? Whom God made you to be? You would be surprised. You can't allow the opinions of other people to validate you. Other people, your friends or family didn't die on a cross for you, neither do they have a heaven or hell to put you in. On judgement day, we all must stand before God and give an account to Him. There will be no excuse of why we weren't whom He called us to be. He has sent Jesus and His Holy

Spirit to help and comfort us along the way, but your heart and soul can refuse the comfort of God. When the pain is cut so deep and thick, it can repel His love.

After experiencing constant neglect and rejection (familial and peer wise) my dreams died inside. I no longer wanted to write, I no longer wanted to write my poetry. No one was listening to me, did anyone care what I had to say? I didn't know how to express myself. I was just taught to suck it up and keep on moving. That was a spiritual attack of the enemy. If you love to write, write unto the glory of God. If you can cook, cook unto the glory of God. If you sing, sing unto the glory of God. The enemy comes to steal, kill and destroy. He knows that you are a weapon against his kingdom once you find out who you really are in Christ and that is what he is afraid of. He will throw spiritual and natural fiery darts to deter you.

The enemy will strategically set up traps and snares to distract you and keep you from moving forward. If you keep your gates open, he will sow seeds of lust, pride, fear, anxiety, worry and much more to contaminate and make you unusable for the kingdom of God. You can't live with one foot in the world and the other foot in church. You can't straddle the fence and serve two masters. Either you are going to go all the way with God or all the way with the devil, because if you are not fully for God, you are against Him.

When the enemy succeeded in keeping me in bondage, I stopped reading to my teddy bears, I stopped reading books. Everything stopped. That was the moment that my spirit died. By this time, I was entering high school and all of my ambition left me. I no longer dreamed, I no longer knew who I was; I was the world's puppet. If you told me to go left, I would go left. If you told me to go right, I would go right. I had no mind of my own, but was controlled and manipulated.

All I wanted was a boyfriend to tell me that he loved me and to validate my already insecure, gullible self. By the time I finished college I experienced many failed relationships and I hit a rock bottom in my life. Now I was depressed. I experienced a nasty heart break. I was chasing after my ex-boyfriend, why? Because he validated me. The very man that I was comfortable with was now taken from me and I felt alone.

I barely had a good night's rest. I lost my job at this point and didn't care. I started to let myself go because I made worldly possessions my idols and they had no substance.

When those idols were taken from me, my foundation was shaken. Now, I'm angry and wanted to be wild. I started going to the club more, drinking, and partying. I wanted a way to release the deep wounds of my heart; I was miserable and so far gone. This can happen when you allow the enemy to torture you because of doubt and unbelief. I knew God's truth, but I choose not to believe. For years and years and years, I sipped tea with the devil.

Wait...what?

Yes, my dear brother or sister reading this. When you choose not to believe God, you walk on the enemy's territory. You are listening to his lies instead of the authenticated truth of God. You choose to believe that you are sad, when God gives you joy. You choose to believe you are worthless, when God counts you precious. You choose to believe that you are clothed in rags, when you are truly clothed in riches. I hear the quote, "From rags to riches." But, I would say that we always were rich, but just choose to be covered in rags. You were always royalty, but just didn't' know it because the enemy used a rag to blind your eyes and mind.

I chose to believe a lie, rather than the truth, because of the great unworthiness that pierced my soul. For the life of me, I could not understand how this God would even take the time out for me. Why do you love me so much, God? Why do you even care? It is because He is our Father. But, I couldn't relate. I had a mother's love, but not a father's love. I wanted to be called princess at 5 years old and wait for my dad to come into the house

with presents. I wanted to be able to call on my dad as a teenager

because my car was broken and I needed help understanding

cars. I wanted to be able to call or text my dad throughout the day

and just say I love you. I wanted my dad to sit me down and tell

me about men, to take me out on my first date and to spend

quality time with him. But, that didn't happen and because it

didn't happen, I blamed my heavenly Father for the lack of my

earthly father's responsibilities.

When my father and my mother forsake me,

Then the Lord will take care of me.

Psalm 27:10

Simply put, God has a love for us that is so astounding that

He sent His one and only Son down from heaven, into the womb

of a virgin named Mary, as a living sacrifice so that we can be

reconciled back to God. Had not Jesus Christ came down in the

flesh and walked this earth to die for us, we would be lost. We

would have no eternal life because sin would have overtaken us.

Jesus was the only man who walked this earth that was SIN-LESS.

Had Christ sinned, He would not have been able to save humanity. It truly amazes me how obedient Jesus was to the Father (God) in fulfilling the purpose God had for His life. Jesus was born to die. That was his life's purpose, to die for us.

He did it so willingly and without mumbling or complaining. How many of us can truly fathom a man who was whipped, beaten, mocked, and hung on a cross for you and I? His blood was shed on the cross like an animal going to the slaughterhouse.

I read about Jesus in amazement sometimes, knowing that his ultimate goal in life wasn't about making a name for himself, having a lucrative career or to make the most money. His goal was to save humanity. We alone in our human strength were not built to carry the heavy burdens of life or to pass through life tied and bound to every circumstance and trial that comes our way. Jesus's ultimate desire in life was to love God with all his heart and mind, and to do the will of God in His life. Jesus loves you with a love that is indescribable and unimaginable. It is only by

Him and through Him that our mere life will ever make sense. This man deserves our full hearts because of what He did for us and continues to do for us every day. It is not by chance you are breathing and living. God touched you this morning and gave you the use and activity of your limbs. You owe Him your life. Jesus Christ is Lord of all, The Holy one of God, is omnipresent, all-powerful, knows everything, is unchanging, has the power to forgive sins, the great high priest, the bring morning star, the Alpha and Omega, the righteous judge, the Messiah, the worthy lamb of God, the good shepherd, the light of the world, the author of life, the prince and savior, the husband of the church, Immanuel, the bread of life, the second Adam and so much more.

He wants the best for you in all areas of your life. Jesus loves you and will never ever leave you. His love is so compelling for us because He believes in us and came to set us free.

In order to rekindle the flame with God, you must return back to the time when you first believed; When God was your everything. Perhaps you never even been in that place. But, you must start from square one. Whenever we receive the free gift of salvation, we are in our infant stages, with childlike manners. Go back to that place and start over. It's time to begin again.

Through Christ, we overcome every obstacle that is thrown our way. We are living in evil and perilous times, plagued by famines, wars, drought, pure evil, murder, strife, broken homes, broken families, corrupt government, prostitution, modern day slavery (human trafficking), sickness, and a host of other alarming conditions. Every time you turn on the news, it is filled with an overbearing sense of negative broadcasts that cause the hair on your arm to stand up straight. Amidst the turmoil of the world, where is that loving peace and restorative mind that so many seek yet fail to receive?

As the times continue to worsen for the world, many of you have been looking for security in your bank account, wealth status, or job; things that can be here today and gone tomorrow. Others are looking for security in broken relationships while others drown themselves in so much work that they have been birthed into a workaholic, losing their sanity along with their ability to "relax" without jumping to the phone every minute to check social media.

"Come to me, all who labor and are heavy laden, and I will give you rest."

Matthew 11:28

Did you hear that? Come to Christ with all of your burdens and weariness. Does your soul need rest? Are you constantly fatigued so much to the point that your days are literally zooming by you before the blink of an eye? Do not put your trust and security in the futility of the world, but place it right at the feet of Christ that simply means to acknowledge Him and acknowledge that you need help. It is okay to need help. Pride is very self-destructive and perhaps you may be dealing with that. Pride is having a total "independent" attitude to the point where you want to be in control of every area of your life, leaving God out of it. God is supposed to lead, and you are supposed to follow.

There is nothing wrong with having your own and becoming financially secure, but don't get too comfortable where you leave God no room to move in your life. Examine yourself and ask whether pride is what has been hindering you today. It is okay to need help and it is okay to ask God for help, direction, and wisdom; that is why He is there.

Psalm 46:1 says that God is an ever-present help in the time of need. Are you in need? Do you need help? What are you turning to for your help? Examine the areas and circumstances of your life where you have tried to do the job of God – that is – taking circumstances in your own hands and have wrecked your brain trying to figure it all out; rather than simply trusting that God will somehow, some way come through.

Your faith will move God, not your emotions. If you have faith the size of a mustard seed, you can say to every mountain to move out of your way (your financial mountains, your relational mountains, your personal mountains) and they have to move! We are more than conquerors. We are above and not beneath, the head and not the tail.

At some point some responsibility has to be taken on our part in seeking God. You have to step out of your comfort zone. You have to do things you haven't normally done in order to get to the place where God wants you to be. You cannot predict God's next move. You will drive yourself crazy trying to analyze every single situation in your life. Simply admit to God that you need help. Be daring and delight in knowing that God is full of surprises. Enjoy this ride with Him.

Do not allow unbelief and pride to keep you from being intimate with God. A Christian walk is birthed by faith. Faith is believing even when you don't have physical evidence in front of you. To accept Christ in your life, you must first BELIEVE that He is Lord and that He rose from the dead. Faith is visualizing it in your mind before actual manifestation occurs. Being prideful hinders you because it tells God that you can do it all by yourself, when you can't. We need God and without him, we are lost.

Like newborn infants, long for the pure, spiritual milk, that by it you may grow up into salvation. (1 Peter 2:2)

Humble yourself and admit that you must start over. When a child comes out of their mother's womb, it is naked. The mother covers and protects that child, warmly wraps the newborn in blankets and feeds the child. That child craves for the milk in order to grow. A screaming child cries when they are hungry, but there are too small and weak to hold the bottle for themselves. Their mother or father must put the bottle in their mouth. Quiet, sucking noises are heard as the newborn is satisfied with its food. We must learn to feed our spiritual (inner) man in order to grow. The pain of life's tribulations and mishaps can stunt our spiritual growth if we refuse to move forward and heal.

We are the newborns that have been born again and our spiritual milk is the word of God. Without it, we can't grow spiritually or mature in Christ. What would happen if a mother doesn't feed her newborn its milk? That child will be malnourished and won't grow. It will have a host of complications because of its deficiency of proper vitamins, supplements and nourishment that this milk provided. As in the natural, so it is in the spiritual

Chapter Four

Regeneration and Restoration

When you are broken for the anointing, it causes you to be uncomfortable in God. There were two types of brokenness that I experienced. The first brokenness was from the pain of life, caused by external circumstances (my father not being around, living conditions, etc.) the second type of brokenness that I experienced was from God humbling me and teaching me how to depend on Him. This brokenness was uncomfortable to my flesh and oftentimes I felt more defeated, than victorious. This brokenness was preparing me for my calling. For many of us have been called, but only a few are chosen.

God has been trying to get your attention for some time now. He has been tugging at your heart and prompting you through your Holy Spirit, but many times we have sent God to voicemail. Have you answered His call? Once you do answer, you will go through constant purging, pruning and humbling in order for the Holy Spirit to conform you to the image of God's Son, Jesus Christ. God will deal with your nasty thoughts, attitudes, lack of submission, pride, potty - mouth and everything else that doesn't look or resemble a holy God.

All that we have acquired in the world (behaviors, mindsets and such) has to be torn down by God, broken off of us so that He can properly rebuild us. It would be better for you to stop resisting, humble and submit yourself unto God and follow His lead. For if you wrestle with God, you are only prolonging the beautiful purpose He has for you and causing more grief on yourself. This walk with God requires intimacy.

God doesn't just want to hear from you on Sunday at church. He wants to know how your day went Monday, what bothered you Tuesday, what you are cooking on Wednesday. He desires to draw so close to you. He wants to be your first priority and to be included on everything that is happing in your life. He is Daddy. He is God. He is your Abba and He desires a closer walk with you. However, that closer walk can only start when you chose to be broken, spiritually naked and unashamed before a

God that knows everything about you anyway.

After all that baggage, after all of that despair, After all that

you go through, something amazing happens. Something

amazing happened to me. God began to touch me, He touched my

heart. At first, I didn't know what to do. Why was I crying to Him

now? Why was I starting to warm up to people again? How can

this be? I was put in an environment where people truly and

authentically loved me and I was so suspicious. You mean to tell

me, you really just want to be my friend? You mean to tell me,

that you support the visions and dreams that God has placed on

the inside of me? Wait, no, this is too good to be true. What is the

catch? What do you want from me? Are you going to talk about

me? What mask do I have to put on today to make you feel good?

But, it wasn't like that this time. Unbeknownst to me, this

new environment was a healing environment for me. No, my

leader and Pastor and sisters and brothers in Christ just wanted to love on me and I didn't know how to receive it. Because I was so bound in the chords of sin, I didn't know how to give nor receive this love. It seemed too good to be true. How could anyone love me? I was so used to pity parties that I would use that as an excuse to stay and sit in my emotions. I would rather believe a lie, than face the truth; because if I faced the truth, I would have to give up my bags that I carried for so long. Facing the truth would mean that I could no longer doubt, but I had to believe.

Facing the truth would force me to actually believe that I was loved and that I could no longer hold onto the past; but the past was my comfort zone that I wallowed in. It felt good to me to sit in my vomit. I was a prisoner in my own mind and self-inflicted cell. The door was wide open, but I choose to stay in that jail cell because freedom didn't seem attainable.

How dangerous.

Sometimes, you can be so used to being mistreated or hurt, that you believe that is the way it is supposed to be. You have been conditioned to deal with pain, sweep it under the rug and

leave it there.

No, I don't want anyone to go into my closet and see what

I'm hiding because then I would have to give up my skeletons.

Those skeletons became a part of me, and were my comfort zone.

But, God came and TURNED MY ENTIRE LIFE AROUND.

So, I began this journey of desiring God and it wasn't easy

at first. You see, your heart is soil and people can sow negative or

positive seeds in that soil which will eventually grow in your life.

It'll grow and be evident in your behaviors, or attitudes. I had so

many deeply rooted and negative seeds that it grew a nasty

harvest in my life; my heart was so cold. You know why? Because

I gave so and so my heart and they broke it. I allowed them to

carry my heart and they gave it back to me shattered.

This was my heart that I trusted you with and you did the

unimaginable with it. So, after years of heartache, I took my heart

back, broken and in pieces and I put it back in my chest. I picked

up every shattered piece with tears in my eyes and tried to piece it together with my glue. Then, with my pieced up heart, I hid it behind the wall where no one could touch it to ever hurt me again.

> *When I was in distress, I sought the Lord;*
> *at night I stretched out untiring hands,*
> *and I would not be comforted.*
>
> **Psalm 77:2**

It was at that time that I shut God out as well. As it is in the natural, so it is in the spiritual realm. I was shutting out people naturally, but doing the same thing to God. Sometimes, we treat God as others have treated us. God is not a man, nor did He do what your father, mother, aunt, grandmother, rapist, molester did to you. You can't keep God in that box and treat Him coldly because of other people's actions. That is where we miss out on His love and healing. So, ask yourself whether the reason why you haven't received your healing has to do with you, or with God?

When God takes those Band Aids off and really gets to the root of our problems, it is weighty, it is hefty, and you are exposed. Whatever spirit that has been in operation to keep you stuck is revealed and doesn't want to leave you because it has housed itself in you for so long; it's a spiritual fight.

I also walked heavily in condemnation. When I would sin, I didn't believe I was truly forgiven. I repented, but still thought about what I did and how unfit for the kingdom of God I was. Since I placed my value and worth in accomplishments and achievements, when I didn't 'accomplish" something from the day, my day had no value to me. I simply wasn't grateful at the fact that this was the day that the Lord has made and I should be rejoicing and be glad in it.

What have you placed your value and worth in? Is it based on how many women are in your call log, late night text messages or how many boyfriends you have, how much money you have in the bank, how many jobs you have? What have you traded your value and worth for? You were worth dying on the cross for. Jesus didn't look at your bank status to see if you were eligible. He didn't look at how many pair of shoes you had when He wanted to redeem your soul from sin. He looked at the imperfect, flaw sinner in us and saw such a great beauty. That's love. How is that? How does God see this magnificent creation when we were covered in filth?

Love sees you for who you really are underneath the dirt and not whom people labeled you as. Then, that same love will clean you up, heal the wounds and restore you as if you were never hurt. His eyesight is different than ours and we must come into agreement with that. Your value and worth is based on God. It comes from Him. You can be completely satisfied in God. Don't believe the lies of the enemy. He is the father of lies and has been lying since the beginning of time. There is absolutely no truth in him and when he comes to try and knock your entire head off, when he comes to steal, kill and destroy, when he comes to take your joy peace, happiness and health; you fight back. You use the weaponry that God has given to you to fight.

So many times we run from God. So many times we keep our negative emotions locked up inside. We don't want to talk about our issues. We are too ashamed. We are worried. We are concerned. We are angry, frustrated, stressed, aggravated, emotional, sad, depressed, overwhelmed, and fatigued. Our heart can become so overwhelmed with the issues of life that it can block out the voice of the Holy Spirit. Now, we can't hear God because we are walking in emotional turmoil and this can lead to further damage.

There were plenty of times when I just wanted to give up. I told God I couldn't do it. I was aggravated. I was irritated. I was frustrated. I was angry inside. I thought some things were unfair; I was not comfortable. God was pushing me, He was stretching me. He was pressing me; His hand was on me heavy. Some days, all I could do was weep, lay on my bed or cry with just enough strength to get my duties done for the day.

I would fall to the ground on my knees, uncertain and afraid. I was afraid and uncertain because I was walking in religion. I truly wasn't trusting God, because if I did, my soul would have been comforted. Perfect love casts out all fear (1 John 4:18)

Where was my life heading? Why weren't things working out? It was in these moments that my soul refused to be comforted. I felt my pain cut too deep. It was in these moments that God was sometimes quiet. He didn't move when I expected Him to. I didn't have anyone to encourage me, I had to learn how to encourage myself in the Lord. I had to learn how to go to my Father and tell Him how I felt, tell Him what upset me, tell Him my innermost secrets. I had to open up to God, because He was there and cares. It was in these moments that I learned humility. I had to be spiritually naked and unashamed in God's eyes. I had to say Lord here I am. This is me.

If God can use me (a once timid, prideful, broken young woman who thought I had no value or worth to birth an international woman's ministry to lead others to Christ,) imagine

what He can do through you! Oh, the possibilities are endless.

Yes, I was broken. Yes I had to overcome trials and tribulations.

However, the day that I decided not to stay hindered is the day

my healing began. I am no longer a prisoner of my past, I am an

overcomer advancing the kingdom of God.

I was being broken for God. I was being purged and it hurt,

it was painful. God taught me that I could not control Him. I

couldn't figure Him out. I just had to trust Him; simply, trust

Him. I didn't have to know everything. The unknown was scary

to me. I wanted to know everything God was doing, when He

was going to do it, how He was going to do it because that made

me feel comfortable. However, when you truly live for God that is

not how He operates. The kingdom of God is a faith, believing

system; childlike faith to be exact. God wants us to simply trust

Him because He is our Father and His word stands true. I will

never forget when God said to me, *"If I tell you everything, how would you learn how to trust me?"* We have to move beyond what we "feel."

Emotions are not bad. God designed emotions, but it's when we live in our emotions, that's what is detrimental. You can feel sad, but don't live in it. You can feel angry, but don't live in it. Discouragements will come, frustration can come. But what will your reaction be when they do come? Once you walk in your emotions, you give those spirits permission to attach itself to you. Then, when you speak out of your mouth about how you "feel" to someone else, you have come into agreement with that spirit. The enemy has no right to touch you unless he has been given permission by God or if you open a spiritual door for him through sin.

Because I fell so many times, it pushed me to have a greater hatred for evil and the enemy. The Son of God has set us free, but our minds can keep us in bondage. Nasty habits, stubbornness, unwillingness to submit and change can keep us locked in our own mental prison cell. God has given us the keys to get out of the prison of sin, but are you still sitting on the bed, waiting to be released? At what moment are we really going to walk effectively in what we were designed to do?

The enemy has been trying to kill and abort your destiny and purpose since you were in the womb. God has spoken greatness over your life and it's up to the enemy to see fit that you never operate in that. Its' not always easy living for God. You are not promised a bed of roses. Yes, God has a great plan for your life, but it comes with sacrifice and obedience.

People acquaint pain with the devil and "feeling good" with God. God allows pain. He allows affliction. Perhaps that is why you find it so easy to run from God when pain comes. Everything is not the devil. Perhaps God needs to strengthen your endurance. Perhaps you have to walk in more humility so God takes away your job, home, or something/someone precious to you. Perhaps you have stubborn ways that need to fall off. Perhaps you need to trust God more, so He dries up your finances. Perhaps you need to pray more, so He causes some tests and trials to come your way. Perhaps you are too busy for Him, so He goes to drastic measures to get your attention.

(Your ways are not our ways)

Perhaps you are called to international ministry, so He needs to prepare you at ground level. You have a testimony. You have a calling. You have purpose and your ministry, calling and purpose have nothing to do with you. It has to do with the souls that are attached to your life. We make everything about us and forget that we are merely the clay and vessels He uses.

You have to be anchored, rooted, and grounded in God to be able to take your stand against the wiles of the enemy. It's time to fight back. It's time to take your rightful place as a child of God. It's time for you to move out of a place of isolation and stagnation and into the place that God has spoken over your life. I had to be broken. You have to be broken out of your own will. It has to be relinquished so God can fully work through you. It's in your broken, low state that you will truly experience the intimacy you need. Walk in your authentic identity.

It's time.

God bless you and Shalom.

Would you like to receive salvation today?

Are you in need of salvation?

If you have never accepted Jesus Christ into your life, please read on.

Jesus is the Lord and Savior to all who confess with their mouth that He is Lord and believe in their heart that God raised Him from the dead. (Romans 10:9 - 10) Christ died to save you. You may ask yourself, what do I need to be saved from? Well, Christ came to save the world from their sins so that we can be put back into right standing with God. Sin separates you from God. Sin is an offense against God - a transgression, a shortcoming, or fault. God hates sin, and us as humans don't have the power to be free from sin without an intervention from God. While we were yet sinners, God didn't hesitate to send His Son Jesus Christ to die on the cross for all, no matter what race, age, or gender you are. God's eyes are upon all of us on earth. He watches with kindness, mercy, compassion, and grace waiting for sinners to come back to Him and start really living the life He has strategically constructed for every individual.

Salvation Prayer

In Jesus name I pray:

Father God in the name of Jesus, I come to you as a sinner repenting of all of my sins. I understand that in you, there is a new life and I am desperate for that change. I ask you to come into my heart right now. According to Romans 10:9-10, you sad that if I confess with my mouth that Jesus is Lord, and believe in my heart that God raised Christ from the dead, I will be saved. Therefore, I make a declaration that Jesus is Lord and I believe whole-heartedly that God raised Christ from the dead. I publicly acknowledge my new commitment to you. Thank you for saving me. Amen.

Rededication

In Jesus name I pray:

Father God, in the name of Jesus, I ask that you forgive me for all of my sins that have separated me from you. Forgive me for backsliding. Lord, I ask you to come into my heart once again and renew a steadfast spirit in me. According to James 4:8, I am drawing near to you, so that you can draw near to me. I believe in your son Jesus Christ and I rededicate my life back to you. From this day forward, I will live for you and strive every day to strengthen my relationship with you. In the name of Jesus Amen.

Anointing

My Letter to God

_____

_____

_____

_____

_____

_____

_____

_____

_____

_____

_____

_____

_____

_____

Broken

Anointing

Broken

Anointing

_____

_____

_____

_____

_____

_____

_____

_____

_____

_____

_____

_____

_____

_____

_____

_____

_____

_____

_____

Broken

Anointing

_____

_____

_____

_____

_____

_____

_____

_____

_____

_____

_____

_____

_____

_____

_____

_____

_____

_____

Broken

Anointing

Broken

Anointing

Broken

Anointing

_____

_____

_____

_____

_____

_____

_____

_____

_____

_____

_____

_____

_____

_____

_____

_____

_____

Broken

Anointing

_____

_____

_____

_____

_____

_____

_____

_____

_____

_____

_____

_____

_____

_____

_____

_____

_____

_____

Broken

Chardoneé Wright

Founder/ CEO

If you received salvation, are interested in scheduling a

workshop or would like to write Chardonee', please email

Bookchardonee@gmail.com

Visit my blog:

www.prompted2pen.wordpress.com

Social Media Outlets:

Facebook Group:

www.facebook.com/groups/Womaniaminc

Facebook Page: www.faceboook.com/womaniamsupportgroup

Website:

www.womaniaminc.com

Twitter:

www.twitter.com/womaniaminc

Instagram: Womaniamct

Youtube: Chardonee' Wright

Broken

36146425R00053

Made in the USA
Middletown, DE
25 October 2016